Baseball: Rules of the Game

Bryant Lloyd

The Rourke Press, Inc.
Vero Beach, Florida 32964

PHOTO CREDITS:
All photos © Lynn M. Stone

EDITORIAL SERVICES:
Penworthy Learning Systems

Library of Congress Cataloging-in-Publication Data

Lloyd, Bryant. 1942
    Baseball: rules of the game / by Bryant Lloyd.
        p. cm. — (Baseball)
    Includes index
    Summary: Surveys the rules of baseball, covering such aspects as strikes, walks, outs, innings, and runs.
    ISBN 1-57103-188-X
    1. Baseball—Rules—Juvenile literature. [1. Baseball—Rules.]
I. Title II. Series: Lloyd, Bryant, 1942-   Baseball.
GV877.L57 1997
796.357'02 ' 022—dc21   97–17456
                                                          CIP
                                                          AC

Printed in the USA

TABLE OF CONTENTS

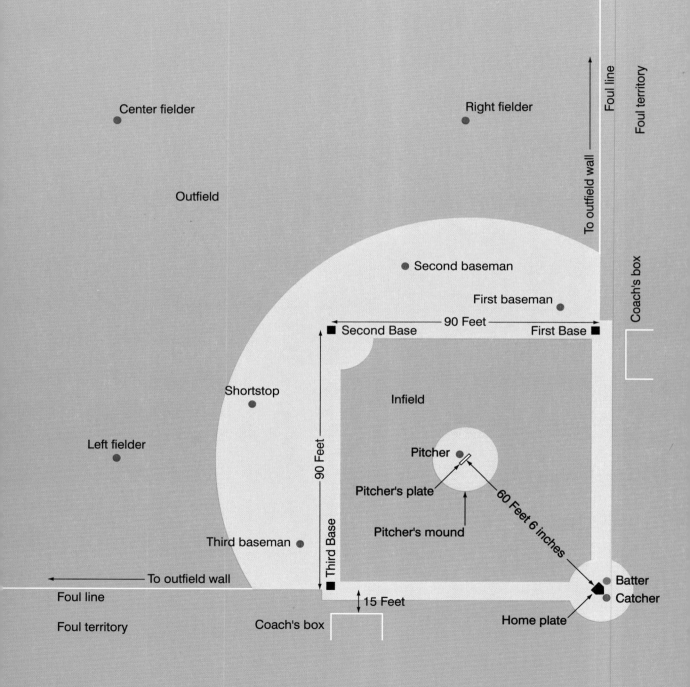

THE PLAYING FIELD

Baseball is played between two teams of nine players each on a mostly flat, fan-shaped field.

The field of play is divided into fair and foul territory and into an outfield and infield. The infield is bounded by four bases.

The base at the point of the infield and fan is home plate. Together, the bases form a diamond shape within the playing field.

The outfield is the area beyond the infield. The end of the outfield is bounded by a fence or wall.

Few girls play baseball, especially after age eight or nine. A similar game to baseball, softball, is very popular with girls. Softball uses a larger, somewhat softer ball and shorter distances between bases than a regulation baseball field.

This diagram shows the basic layout of a professional baseball field.

THE TEAMS

One team of nine players called the **defense** (DEE fents) plays in the field. The other team is "at bat." A visiting team always bats first.

The batting team sends one player at a time to bat. That player is the batter. Batters follow an order decided by a coach.

Expecting a hitter to bunt, the defense's third baseman (right) and first baseman (left) rush forward as the pitcher throws to the plate.

A batter takes a "cut" during a Little League game.

The team at bat uses batters in its lineup, each taking a turn. Each batter either makes an out or reaches a base. Only a team at bat—the **offensive team** (aw FEN siv TEEM)—can score.

THE PITCHER AND CATCHER

One of the nine defensive players is the pitcher. From a low dirt mound across from home plate, the pitcher throws the baseball to a teammate called the catcher. In a regulation baseball game, the pitcher throws a distance of 60-1/2 feet (about 18 meters).

The catcher crouches behind home plate. The batter stands next to the plate. A batter may swing and hit the ball, or choose to let the pitch go by to the catcher.

The catcher waits for the pitch as the batter prepares to swing at it.
The umpire crouches behind the catcher for a good look at the pitch.

STRIKES

Each pitch by the pitcher is either hit by the batter or counted as a **ball** (BAWL) or **strike** (STRYK). If three strikes are recorded, the batter is out and must leave the plate. Balls hit into foul territory also count as strikes—but not as a third strike.

The **strike zone** (STRYK ZONE) is the area over the plate and between a batter's shoulders and knees. A strike is counted if a pitched ball passes through the strike zone and is not hit. A strike is also called if a batter swings at a pitch— any pitch—and misses it.

Little League games are scheduled for six innings. Major League games are scheduled for nine innings. High school games may be seven or nine innings. Most college games are nine innings.

A batter watches the pitch sail by belly high, but chooses not to swing. The umpire will decide if the pitch was inside or outside the plate area.

STRIKEOUTS AND WALKS

Batters on whom three strikes are recorded, strike out. Pitchers like to get strikeouts, but they don't like **walks** (WAWKS).

The batter steps back—quickly!—from a tight, inside pitch.

This swing popped the ball up and behind batter—a foul ball. It counts as a first or second strike—but not a third except on a bunt attempt.

Pitches not hit that miss the strike zone are called balls by the **umpire** (UM pyr). A batter who takes four pitches called balls earns a "base on balls" or a "walk." The batter who walks goes to first base, becoming a base runner without hitting the baseball.

FIELDERS

The pitcher and catcher are fielders. Fielders are defense players in the field. Their job is to catch the baseball when it is hit by a batter.

Other infielders include a first baseman, second baseman, shortstop, and third baseman. The three outfielders are the left, center, and right fielders. Sometimes a team will move an infielder into the outfield as a fourth outfielder.

Professional baseball games are played for nine innings (or more) regardless of score. In nonprofessional leagues, a "mercy rule" can stop a one-sided game, usually after five innings, and if one team leads by 10 or more runs.

A fielder never wants to make a lazy throw to a base. A throw with oomph! like this fielder's toss, has a much better chance of beating the runner.

OUTS

A strike out is one way for a batter to make an out. The team at bat is allowed three outs each time a player bats.

A batter is out if a fielder catches a ball hit in the air. Many outs occur by balls hit on the ground—ground balls. An infielder can pick up the ground ball and throw it to first base. If the throw reaches the first baseman's glove before the batter's foot touches first base, the batter is out.

The race is on! If the shortstop's throw to the first baseman beats the runner's attempt to reach base before the ball, the runner is out. First baseman, though, must have a foot on base when catching the ball.

INNINGS

A batter who reaches first, second, or third base safely is a base runner. Teams get ready to score runs by having base runners. A base runner can be out, however, when the next batter hits. A fielder can throw to the base the original runner is trying to reach. If the throw beats the runner, or the fielder tags the runner, that player is out.

A runner reaches second base safely, ahead of the throw that draws the shortstop off base.

A good fielder is always alert and in position ready for the next batter.

After the first team to bat makes three outs, one way or another, a half inning has been played. After the other team bats and makes three outs, a full inning has been played.

RUNS

The goal in a baseball game is to score more runs than the other team.

A run is scored when a base runner reaches home plate safely after touching the other three bases.

A **home run** (HOME RUN) is a hit ball that flies out of the playing field in fair territory. Any players who might have been on base score ahead of the home run hitter.

The player who hit the "homer" scores immediately after running from one base to the next.

The great popularity of baseball resulted in its being called the "National Pastime" many years ago. Children can begin organized baseball as early as age five.

A smooth, level swing helps batters hit home runs and drive other runners across home plate with runs.

GLOSSARY

ball (BAWL) — a pitch at which a batter does not swing and that does not pass through the batter's strike zone

defense (DEE fents) — the team on the field trying to stop batters from scoring

home run (HOME RUN) — a four-base hit in which, usually, the batter drives the ball in fair territory out of the baseball park

offensive team (aw FEN siv TEEM) — the team at bat and trying to score

strike (STRYK) — a pitch that is swung at and missed or hit into foul territory; also a pitch thrown into the strike zone and not swung at

strike zone (STRYK ZONE) — the area over the plate and between the batter's shoulders and knees

umpire (UM pyr) — any one of the officials on the field who makes decisions about the game, such as fair or foul, ball or strike

walk (WAWK) — to make four pitches called balls by the umpire to one batter; a base on balls

An umpire makes sure baseball game is played according to rules, and home plate is kept tidy!

INDEX